D1282212

MIKE
Box 4461 FSM
32306

# FREEDOM OF THE MIND

## By William O. Douglas

FREEDOM OF THE MIND

THE ANATOMY OF LIBERTY

MR. LINCOLN AND THE NEGROES

DEMOCRACY'S MANIFESTO

MY WILDERNESS: EAST TO KATAHDIN

A LIVING BILL OF RIGHTS

MY WILDERNESS: THE PACIFIC WEST

AMERICA CHALLENGED

WEST OF THE INDUS

THE RIGHT OF THE PEOPLE

RUSSIAN JOURNEY

WE THE JUDGES

AN ALMANAC OF LIBERTY

NORTH FROM MALAYA

BEYOND THE HIGH HIMALAYAS

STRANGE LANDS AND FRIENDLY PEOPLE

OF MEN AND MOUNTAINS

BEING AN AMERICAN

# FREEDOM OF THE MIND

*William O. Douglas*

DOUBLEDAY & COMPANY, INC.
GARDEN CITY, NEW YORK
1964

105583

This book is one of the series "Reading for an Age of Change," published by the American Library Association, 50 East Huron Street, Chicago 11, Illinois, and distributed by Public Affairs Committee, 22 East 38th Street, New York 16, New York.

IN 1962 a senior in an eastern preparatory school was forbidden to deliver his valedictory address because it was "pink" and "dangerous." According to the press reports of June 5 the speech called on the United States to work for disarmament and listed four moves we could make to achieve disarmament:

"Stop all nuclear tests, underground, underwater, in the atmosphere, and in space.

"End all production of nuclear weapons and delivery systems.

"Disarm all bases on foreign soil of nuclear weapons.

"Mothball all Polaris-firing submarines.

"The speech said the four proposals would not 'seriously impair our retaliatory capacity.'

"It said that if the Russians would not agree to disarmament with inspection after the plan was initiated, this country still would have time to rearm.

"'It is our duty as the leading nation of the Western World to prove to the Russians that we want peace, not say we want peace, but prove it, for time is quickly running out,' [the senior] said in the speech.

"'Neither Russia nor America wants war for they have reached the point at which the possible gains of such a war are far outweighed by the destruction that it would bring. Each side has too much to lose.'"

How could a Free Society reach a point where anyone in authority would bar this utterance, however worthless he might think it to be?

## The trend to conformity

The trend to conformity has possessed us since World War II. The causes are numerous, some of them reflecting no more than a conservative outlook that is usually reflected in an affluent society. But there are other reasons.

One leveling influence has been the scientific revolution. Technology has become a rather dubious synonym for progress; man has become more and more subordinate to the machine. The arrival of a new labor-saving device is hailed as an achievement, though it displaces more men and women. Work is an important therapy. What will take its place? Is man doomed to live a life of enervative leisure?

We have a surplus of everything—including unemployed people; and the hundreds of unemployed and unemployable will increase if technology continues to be our master. We have a surplus of food and millions of hungry people at home as well as abroad.

When the machine displaces man and does most of the work, who will own the machines and receive the rich dividends? Are we on the threshold of re-entering the world of feudalism which Europe left in the 15th and 16th centuries and which is fastened on much of the Middle East today?

The new centers of power are in the hands of those who control science; and one who traces the controls back to origins often finds the Pentagon in the central position. Those who finance the scientific revolution usually control those who work for them. The impact of this control on our universities is so great that their autonomy is threatened.

There is ample evidence that our colleges and universities have become citadels of anti-radicalism. One who sits on the sidelines and listens to the highly factual, unimaginative, and tranquilizing essays they produce sometimes concludes that he is a witness to an inquest. Yet if planning in this fast-moving age of technology is not being designed in university circles, from what source will it come?

Investigating committees of Congress and state legislatures invade the campus and examine teachers for their "loyalty." Badges of "communism" have been pinned on teachers, not because they were presently members of the party but because they once had been, or because they had joined causes that the party had promoted, or because they were members of other organizations into which Communists had infiltrated.

These investigations have not been restricted, of course, to teachers; they covered government employees, trade union members, dock workers, workers in factories having contracts with the government, radio and TV employees, movie actors and actresses, reporters for newspapers, and any organization having a relation to communications, transportation, or production that was directly or indirectly related to national "security."

These investigations have a powerful impact on those who make policy decisions on foreign relations. People in positions where inventive genius is desirable become conformists. Those removed from office, those who voluntarily relinquish their posts rather than go through the expense and agony of hearings, even those who face the ordeal and disprove the charges, have often been tagged with the same label. The publicity of the accusation is seldom forgotten. It always reaches the headlines, while any clearance is seldom deemed newsworthy.

These episodes telegraph themselves to younger people preparing for their careers, as well as to those already in the ranks. Conformity appears to be the only safe course. During the period of the 1940's and early 1950's the registration in Russian language courses dropped precipitately. What better evidence that a youngster was "Communist" than the fact that he or she was studying Russian? During this period, those who needed Russian materials for Russian language or history courses were suspect. Pressures were put on college authorities by the postal service not to accept deliveries from Russia. That happened, for example, in New York State. During the period the F. B. I. was careful to check visitors from Communist countries who put foot on a college campus. "Who was responsible for bringing that Polish professor to the University?" was the inquiry of the F. B. I. to university authorities in more than one state. Such surveillance is not consistent with academic freedom.

The rash of loyalty oaths also has had a deadening effect on freedom of inquiry. People in most ranks are required to swear that they never have been members of any "subversive" organization. Most people who have not been members readily take the oath. Others who have not been members stubbornly refuse. Why? That kind of oath—as distinguished from one that promises future loyalty—seems to some conscientious people to be a meddling that is none of government's rightful concern. Government, they maintain, may examine a person for fitness. But what possible relevancy to fitness to teach mathematics, say, is an innocent mistake made thirty years earlier? Or for that matter, what relevancy is past "knowing" membership? Moreover, do not redemption and forgiveness have a place in our values?

It is along these general lines that the battle for conformity has been waged in and out of courts. It still goes on. People today, like people hundreds of years ago, insist that one of their inalienable rights is to be let alone *except and unless* they violate some constitutional law. To many the right to defy an unconstitutional law is the citizen's prerogative. See Douglas, *The Right of the People,* pp. 158 *et seq.* No law is constitutional, they assert, that makes one take a "test oath" which probes the past for conduct, lawful when done. The right of privacy, they maintain, is the essence of the First Amendment.

Those who take that position stand more and more alone. The majority for fear of their jobs, for lack of conviction on grounds of principle, or for ignorance of the stakes involved go along. Very few speak up for the small minority. Even lawyers retreated, until a "test" oath was proposed for them.

There have been "black" lists and "gray" lists. The "black" list is made up of those who have been summoned before an investigating committee and labeled a past or present member of the Communist party; the "gray" list is made up of those who refuse to sign a loyalty oath. In the movie industry, those on either list may be writers, camera men, stage hands, actors. They stand condemned because of some prior action that associated them with communism, because of their disbelief in loyalty oaths, or because actually they are Communists. Yet how can political ideology be relevant to the job of a camera man, or a stage hand, or an actor? One can say that a writer may try to infiltrate Communist ideology into a script. Is not that dangerous? some will ask. But it is the producer and director who determine what goes on the screen. Though the writer tries to give the script an ideological slant, it is never his responsibility to decide what is screened.

The result is that the awesome power of governmental groups has been brought to bear on that segment of the press represented by the movies. That power is used to tell the industry whom they may not employ. Similar efforts have been made to get some newspapers not to retain employees because they once had been or presently are members of the party.

As the search for the "subversive" in our midst proceeded, its definition was gradually expanded to include more than active members of a conspiracy against the established order. It was expanded to include members of organizations into which Communists had infiltrated, and finally individuals and members of organizations that supported causes which the Communists supported, such as the civil war against Franco in Spain. Those classifications gained validity in the public mind by activities of legislative investigating committees, by state and federal laws, and by judicial opinions. The image of the "subversive" was projected into the international field, with the result that even passionate advocates of the Free Society, such as Nehru, became "dangerous" because they were socialist in political philosophy, because they were soft-spoken *vis-à-vis* Soviet Russia or often voted with her in the U. N.

## A sense of insecurity

Most of these restraints on liberty, which we have witnessed, flowered because of the sense of insecurity that pervaded this society following World War II; and the press and pulpit have done very little to put the internal Communist threat into perspective.

Communism is real; communism is virulent; country after country was overrun by it—by invading armies, not by the electoral process; in exploited nations like Cuba, not in advanced societies such as France and Italy. But the spectre grows.

Communism became a prime political slogan. The realities of communism and the reasons for its success in areas where it succeeded were not discussed. The defeats suffered by communism, as in Egypt, India, Iraq, and Israel, were hardly noticed. The "test" oath became a way of making A seem politically more reliable than B, who is "soft" on communism; A, who is not "soft," becomes the ideal; and in the political forum everyone tries to prove by word and deed that he is like A, not like B. And so the goose-stepping march of conformity is joined by more and more people. The voice of dissent becomes feeble. The unorthodox borders on the treasonable. The free exchange of ideas diminishes; public debate falls off; the nation moves more and more to the right; leftist thought, so important in American history, almost disappears; a great polarization of political thought to the center and to the right of center takes place.

All of these things might have happened, even if we were not an affluent society. Being members of one, we became more and more wedded to the *status quo*. The *status quo* at home seems symbolic of the *status quo* everywhere, though in truth the *status quo* in many nations is a cruel oppressive thing. But since we are unused to unorthodox views at home, we are painfully ill at ease abroad and telegraph our insecurity to sensitive minds across the globe. The image of America changes. We seem afraid of freedom —for other peoples as well as for ourselves. We are robbed of our greatest strength, which is in our ideas. Ideas are of course dangerous. Yet by reason of the Bill of Rights we put our faith in their full and free expression. Our abandonment of that faith has taken a heavy toll.

## Mass communications

Another leveling influence is the nature of mass communication. The press, radio, and television for the sake of money aim to reach an ever-widening audience. That means finding the lowest common denominator. The tendency is to skip the controversial or touch it only lightly. As a result, the public communication system since World War II has not filled its traditional role of informing and educating as Lacy, in *Freedom and Communications*, shows.

Americans have been alarmed at the unorthodoxy in the world and remain quite unaware of the *Five Ideas That Change the World* as told by Barbara Ward. The vast efforts of news-gathering agencies often fail to bring much enlightenment. The majority of foreign news—as high as 80 per cent—is not put on the wires when it reaches this country, and the American appetite for the remaining 20 per cent is not great. One who reads only his local paper will, in all probability, grow up without an understanding of the present-day world. Much of the overseas news that reaches home is not reliable. Our newsmen who travel the world seldom speak the local language and therefore are in large degree only propagandists for special interests that have their ear. They do not on their own feel the pulse of the villages.

The increasing complexity of modern life also causes a proliferation in news that makes it difficult for any publication to keep abreast. The actual forces at work in any one foreign nation, say in Indonesia, require reporting in depth that very few publications can afford.

There are now over 100 nations in the United Nations. The interpretation of their voices, a fair appraisal of their motives, an understanding of their problems require an expertness that few Americans have. There are official information agencies that supply a mass of press releases which attempt to explain certain events or to justify certain policies of this government and of other governments. The tendency is to take one or two or three of these press releases as the gospel and look no further. That is the easiest course and the safest one. The result is that much news dealing with foreign affairs only repeats parrot-like what the press releases say, without any real effort to probe beneath the surface. The result is a voice of conformity on foreign affairs when nonconformity at times would be the greatest public service.

The growing perplexity of modern affairs has also made it more and more difficult to have informed reporting.

Outer space is a specialty of vast proportions. Nuclear energy and the dangers of its peaceful use are known only to a select few. The federal budget has become so complex that not many penetrate its mysteries. The Corps of Army Engineers often allocates funds to other agencies to do its research work. The manner in which that kind of budget manipulation is used to create "captive agencies" is known largely only to insiders. The agency that has "captive agencies" controls most of those experts who could criticize it but dare not. So its plans and projects go largely uncriticized and it becomes a "sacred white cow."

An establishment such as the Pentagon is so vast that probably no one except a few members of the Senate and the House comprehend it. Its annual budget—which is now greater than the annual income of the 600 million Chinese under the Peking regime —sustains a vast propaganda machine as well as armies. It is heavily involved in such things as conservation at home and village "reform" programs abroad. It has its own built-in state department that is never in the public eye but that shapes policies. The Secretary of State is the voice that is heard; but the true policy-forming group is often the Pentagon's political bureaus—all this being contrary to our theory of the supremacy of the civilian authority over the military. See Gellhorn, *American Rights; the Constitution in Action.*

The press does not cover the operations of the Pentagon adequately. Nor can it report truthfully on the Central Intelligence Agency. This agency has been more responsible than any other agency for foreign policy in the Middle East. Its movements are not known. The manner in which it intercedes in foreign elections with its moneybags is never reported. The reasons why it supports feudal regimes, the results of its policies, the dangers that it generates are not known even to many of the informed press.

Secrecy of C. I. A. and Pentagon operations is defended on grounds of national security; and obviously matters of espionage and counterespionage, as well as many matters of defense, cannot be successful if they are news items. Yet why should the C. I. A. efforts to influence elections abroad be a secret to the American people when they are notorious in the foreign nation?

This matter of secrecy of government information is a never-ending controversy. Every person in power and every party in power has an impulse or desire to conceal or minimize failures and to advertise achievements. If failures can be easily "swept under the rug," life in government becomes easier. Reasons for secrecy are often valid ones. Delicate diplomatic negotiations would be jeopardized if made public. Yet the secrecy that enveloped the atomic bomb project in World War II has been the pattern for projects far less worthy. As Wiggins in *Freedom or Secrecy* says, the purpose of the First Amendment's guarantee of freedom of speech and press is not merely to let people blow off steam. Foremost is the public's right to know. For the people are sovereign. How their government should be run is their business. If they lack the knowledge, they will not exercise the franchise intelligently.

When it comes to commercial matters many subtle forces also operate to keep us in step with some conformist tune. Products advertised on radio and TV are the lifeblood of broadcasting. They are dressed in attractive Madison Avenue garb and sold in mass. Some are dangerous to health. Yet the facts concerning them, notably insecticides, are never disclosed to the public, as Rachel Carson says in her book *Silent Spring*. Detergents with a carbon molecule are insoluble and do not break down under the bacterial action of sewage disposal systems. The detergents enter even the percolating waters of artesian wells and we drink them. Five hundred new insecticides come out every year, some of them lethal. No agency, no press, no radio or TV reports on their dangers. To report would be to lose advertisers; and so the people are kept in the dark concerning the "poisons" in every meal we eat. The voices of public health officials are either quiet or timid. Why? Their budgets are low; they lack funds for necessary research. The chemical companies are formidable foes; they not only have powerful political alliances, they help educate the entomologists who in turn become their spokesmen or defenders. They have corrupted some educational institutions in the manner that lumber companies have corrupted some forestry schools.

This was the climate in which most of the press prospered since World War II. They stayed quiet on issues that would disturb advertisers. They prospered by spreading alarms about Communists at home and abroad. Their editorial pages were cudgels against officeholders or candidates who had a different view. They used their pressures against nonconformists in schools, colleges, and universities.

There are exceptions among the press. Atlanta, Boston, Denver, Little Rock, Louisville, Memphis, New York City, Providence, Sacramento, St. Louis, and Washington, D.C. have a different kind of press—newspapers that take on controversial issues and are never cowed, no matter how prominent and influential the opposition. By and large, however, the guarantee of freedom of the press is exploited not as an educational force but as a money-making project.

Dr. Robert M. Hutchins of the Center for the Study of Democratic Institutions recently said in *The Political Animal:*

"Suppose that the media of mass communication were really on their toes. They would have no difficulty in bringing the military to book. Only *The Nation* as far as I know—or

*The New Republic,* perhaps—has tried to do this in any consistent way, and their circulations are remarkably and unfortunately small. But suppose that any one of the wire services or any major newspaper in the United States, or any group of them, really went after the relationship of the military to the public policies of this country—I do not believe that there would be any difficulty in bringing the military to book.

"The constitutional provisions are clear. The tradition of this country about the supremacy of the civilian power over the military power is clear. I am sure that the general attitude of the people would be most unfriendly to the assumption of autocratic or arbitrary or comprehensive power on the part of the military. The Secretary of Defense has encountered no really serious opposition to the efforts that he has made, some of them quite significant, to bring the military under civilian control.

"In short, the predominance of the military results from the apathy and ignorance of the people. The people are ignorant because they are uninformed. I think they are apathetic because they are uninformed. If the media were really on their job, this phenomenon that we see and to which President Eisenhower referred could not long exist."

Dr. Hutchins is, in my view, correct in his estimate of the unused power of the press. Moreover, if the press were alert, if the press were functioning in its historic way, our breakfasts, luncheons, and dinners would not be seasoned with the "poisons" now so prevalent. The press could, if it would, correct the appalling condition which Rachel Carson discusses in *Silent Spring.*

This decline in the educative role of the press has resulted in a decline in freedom. If the press would serve its traditional role, there would be a real awakening in America. Without that awakening, we will not have the courage and imagination to deal with forces at home and abroad that are increasingly complex and increasingly dangerous.

## The Bill of Rights

The American government is premised on the theory that if the mind of man is to be free, his ideas, his beliefs, his ideology, his philosophy must be placed beyond the reach of government. In theory he can be the minority of one that John Stuart Mill talked about and yet go unpunished for what he thinks. In theory, he can keep his thoughts to himself, respect confidences, and not be compelled by government to open his mouth. Freedom of belief—in a certain kind of God or in a certain kind of social order—was placed in sacred precincts that government could not enter. What one advocates, the nature of the religious, political, moral, economic, or social order which he would impose on the world, were he ruler—these are none of government's concerns. The individual is sovereign and none can punish him for his convictions nor for the manner in which he proselytizes his cause. Konvitz, *Fundamental Liberties of a Free People*, states the basic philosophy.

In theory, government should be interested only in conduct, in overt acts. Speaking, advocating, praying—like thinking and believing—are beyond the reach of laws. Government should take action only when ideas are translated into action, when speaking crosses the line of advocacy and enters the realm of nudist shows, acts of perversion, riots, parades, distribution of guns, formation of military units, espionage, or other types and forms of overt acts which are made illegal by legislative action.

This theory was expressed in various ways. *The Federalist* emphasized the importance of preserving and protecting each minority:

"In a free government the security for civil rights must be the same as that for religious rights. It consists in the one case in the multiplicity of interests, and in the other in the multiplicity of sects."

As stated by Jefferson in 1786 ". . . it is time enough for the rightful purposes of civil government for its office to interfere when principles break out into overt acts against peace and good order."

A whole congeries of constitutional provisions was adopted in protection of the *freedom of the mind.*

Article VI of the Constitution provides:

". . . no religious test shall ever be required as a Qualification to any Office or public Trust under the United States."

Article III, Section 3 narrowly defines treason:

"Treason against the United States, shall consist only in levying War against them or in adhering to their Enemies, giving them Aid and Comfort. No Person shall be convicted of Treason unless on the Testimony of two Witnesses to the same overt Act, or on Confession in open Court."

Once upon a time *legislatures* convicted people for their political ideology as well as for their actions by measures known as bills of attainder. Article I, Sections 9 and 10, of the Constitution prohibits the federal government and the states respectively from enacting them.

If people are to be convicted, they must be charged by a grand jury and tried before judge and jury, not by a legislature.

At one time thoughts, beliefs, or acts—wholly legal when they occurred—could be made retroactively illegal. Article I, Sections 9 and 10, of the Constitution prohibits that kind of law by banning any *ex post facto* legislation.

The First Amendment gives protection in terms that are absolute to religion, speech, press, assembly, and petition:

"Congress shall make no law respecting an establishment of religion, or prohibiting the free exercise thereof; or abridging the freedom of speech, or of the press; or the right of the people peaceably to assemble, and to petition the Government for a redress of grievances."

Other provisions of the Bill of Rights bear tangentially on the freedom of the mind. Thus the Fourth Amendment guarantees the "right of the people to be secure in their persons, houses, papers, and effects against unreasonable searches and seizures" by providing that no warrant should be issued except by a magistrate on a showing of "probable cause" that particularly describes "the place to be searched and the persons or things to be seized."

The Fifth Amendment prescribes the manner in which a criminal charge may be leveled against a person. It must be by a presentment or indictment of a grand jury.

As a corollary the Fifth Amendment provides that "no person . . . shall be compelled in any criminal case to be a witness against himself"—a method of accusation once used in lieu of a presentment or indictment, as Chafee, *The Blessings of Liberty* explains.

The Sixth Amendment describes how a person shall be tried in a criminal prosecution. He has the right to an impartial jury; he must have the assistance of counsel and the right to summon witnesses; he must be informed of "the nature and cause of the accusation"; he is entitled "to be confronted with the witnesses against him."

The foregoing provisions of the Bill of Rights—the First, Fourth, Fifth, and Sixth Amendments—were originally applicable only to the federal government. After the Civil War the Fourteenth Amendment was adopted and it provides that no state shall "deprive any person of life, liberty, or property without due process of law." A long-term argument has taken place as to the meaning of "due process." Some maintain that "due process" as used in the Fourteenth Amendment makes the Bill of Rights applicable to the states. That view to date has not prevailed, though more than nine Justices, starting with the first Mr. Justice Harlan, have thought so. The Court has, however, selectively incorporated the provisions of the first eight amendments into the "due process" clause of the Fourteenth.

The First Amendment and the Fourth Amendment are now held to be applicable to the states as well as to the federal government. The Self-Incrimination Clause of the Fifth Amendment has been partially applied to the states as follows: the Court has held that though the failure of an accused to testify at a state trial or state hearing can be used against him, the Self-Incrimination Clause of the Fifth Amendment prohibits the police or prosecutor of a state from using torture or other methods of coercion to force him to make self-incriminating statements.

These are the main constitutional safeguards of freedom of the mind in America. Words, however, do not always have the meaning which seems apparent on the surface. Their historic setting and the *apologia* written by judges are needed to explain, if not to understand, the manner in which freedom of the mind has at times been more illusory than real even in this Free Society. See Fellman, *The Limits of Freedom*.

## Shackles on thought

"Thou Shalt Not" (a recurring slogan throughout recorded history) has been used by each age to shackle the mind and put severe restraints on freedom of inquiry. Theologians of almost every school have thought, as Francis Bacon wrote long ago, that "too much knowledge should incline a man to atheism." Ignorance was fostered by prelates so that their flocks would not have doubts of the supernatural as explained by the prelates. Keeping the masses ignorant was the political policy of rulers who wanted silent acquiescence rather than unrest and change.

The theologians and rulers were often one and the same, the state existing in order to support and propagate one religious creed. One of the modern examples was Outer Mongolia which was conquered by China in 1691. China's desire was to keep Outer Mongolia subdued so that China's backdoor would be secure. To achieve that end she turned over the management of the country to Buddhist lamaseries. These multiplied until they absorbed half of the male population. They kept all education within their walls. Only lamas could read and write; only lamas had medical services. The rest of the people lived and died in ignorance of the nature of sunrises and sunsets, of electric storms, and without medical care. They also knew nothing of the industrial revolutions, for the outside world had been sealed off from them. This condition continued until July 11, 1921, when the Mongolians at last broke the bonds and won their independence from China.

Modern examples of that extreme character are not common, though church control in some nations has approximated the same condition; and an analogous situation prevails in South Africa.

The arrival of the printing press and the vast paraphernalia for publishing and distributing books and other literature spread ideas across the world. More and more people learned to read and, having acquired knowledge, sought to spread it. And so the major contest since the printing press has been over what may be published and distributed, what may be read and transmitted by the spoken word, and even what may be believed or thought.

The matter of belief has created some of the bloodiest chapters of history. Kings, sitting on uneasy thrones, always sought out the "subversives" amongst their people. Those who schemed and plotted against the king, collecting arms, making plans for riots, assassinations, and seizure of government arsenals, were of course punished for their overt acts. But what of those sullen, silent people who wished the king were dead but never put their wishes into action? What greater uneasiness is there than that created by a host of enemies who have not moved into action but may do so? The law—which was usually the instrument of the ruler—designed a method of reaching this "subversive" group.

British law made it a treasonable crime to "compass or imagine the death of the King," the crime known as constructive treason. This crime was borrowed from Dionysius (430–367 B. C.) who executed a subject for dreaming he had killed him. That was sufficient proof, Dionysius said, that the subject had thought about killing him when he was awake.

Jefferson said that his crime of constructive treason "had drawn the blood of the best and honestest men in the Kingdom." Men were indeed executed merely for uttering treasonable words. In 1351 the British Parliament, while retaining as one definition of treason, the compassing and imagining the death of the King, ameliorated the plight of the suspects by requiring that there be an overt act. In other words, wishing that the King were dead was not enough. Doing something about it was necessary. The deed, rather than the thought alone, became a necessary ingredient of the crime of treason. But reducing treasonable words to writing was considered an overt act. The ease with which the concept of an overt act was expanded resulted in the American narrow definition, *viz:* "only in levying war" against the United States "or in adhering to their Enemies, giving them aid and comfort." Since, moreover, the treasonable act might be only a drummed-up charge, the Framers of our Constitution provided that in order for a charge of treason to be proved, it was necessary to have two witnesses to each overt act.

While kings were fearful of treason, theologians were bent on stamping out heresy. One of the charges against Socrates was "impiety"—that is to say, he denied the existence of the gods that had been recognized by the state. Every religion at some time and place has been denounced as heresy; and those in power have tried to put it down. Sects within Christianity have shown the same intolerance. The Reformation is associated with Martin Luther. But prior to him it broke out many times only to be crushed. When in time the Protestants gained control, they tried to crush the Catholics; and when the Catholics gained the upper hand, they ferreted out the Protestants. Many devices were used. Heretical books were destroyed and heretics were burned at the stake or banished. Those charged with the crime of printing books without a license and those charged with heresy were required to take the oath *ex officio*.

The oath *ex officio* made unnecessary an indictment, trial by jury, and confrontation of accusing witnesses. The judge *ex officio, i. e.* by virtue of his office as judge, summoned the party to court on suspicion, on probable cause, or on whim or caprice, and instituted action against him. It was this practice of requiring the accused to testify or to go to jail for contempt that was ended in England by Act of Parliament in 1368. After that a presentment or indictment was necessary to require a man to answer. But that obtained only in the King's Courts. The ecclesiastical courts and the notorious Star Chamber continued to use the oath *ex officio*. The Puritans learned that this was the most awesome power the government had over them. It was used to make them follow objectionable religious ceremonies, to punish them for speech and thought, and to ferret out the nonconformists who surreptitiously published "dangerous" tracts. Thus experience overseas brought to these shores bitterness against devices that forced men to convict themselves against conscience and dignity out of their own mouths. Chafee in *The Blessings of Liberty* gives a faithful account of the use of the oath *ex officio* against John Udall in 1589 and John Lilburn in 1647—trials touching freedom of the press that were burned into the memories of the American colonists.

Theologians could bring their full wrath down on heretics only if they had secular power. Once the theologians manned the courts, controlled the legislators, and picked the prosecutors, the way of the heretic was hard. A struggle for political control became a struggle for control by a religious group. The excesses were so great, the divisions within society created by religious differences were so deep that union of church and state was banned by the First Amendment.

That meant that government could not meddle in religious affairs either by establishing a church or a religious ritual or ceremony, or by interfering with the individual's free exercise of religion. Conversely it meant that no sect could run government to serve its ends, nor have taxes levied for religious purposes, nor make laws requiring a person to observe any particular religious ritual. Moreover, as already noted, there was included within the main body of the Constitution a provision that no religious test should ever be required for public office; and that provision has been held to be so broad as to make it unconstitutional to bar atheists from public office.

The medieval church concerned itself with heresy, not with obscenity. Obscene literature went largely unpoliced and unpunished through ancient Greece, ancient Rome, and well into the 16th century in England. By the mid-16th century Puritanism had gained the ascendancy and under its aegis bawdy books, songs, and plays were banned. Licensing the press, which appeared in England before the mid-16th century, was mainly used to suppress heretical writings, and was only feebly aimed at obscene publications. Licensing the press ended with the 17th century. But in 1727 English judges made publishing an obscene work a crime "as it tends to corrupt the morals of the King's subjects." It is largely from that theme that the modern law of obscenity derives.

## Libel laws

As noted, the crime of "treason" as it evolved concerned wartime activities of disloyalty. Seditious libel did service for treason in times of peace. Criminal libel was a branch of seditious libel. Defamation was made a crime because of its tendency to cause a breach of the peace; and for that reason it was a species of sedition. It is present today in most states and is defined as "malicious defamation" that either impeaches the "virtue" of a person or tends to bring him into "public ridicule." In practice criminal libel is not frequently used, and today has no relation to sedition or to the overthrow of government by unlawful means. It was once used to punish a man who exposed the memory of George Washington to obloquy. It more frequently punishes those who vilify a minority. Vilification of a minority reached its historic peak with Hitler's propaganda against the Jews; and so criminal libel is justified today. Vituperative utterances may, in their setting, be "fighting words" that are so closely related to the outbreak of violence as to be part and parcel of the overt act.

In England seditious libel and criminal libel assumed such large dimensions that they were threats to everyone active in public affairs. Those who criticized the regime in power might be prosecuted either for seditious libel or for criminal libel. Private groups, if they had friends in court, could launch prosecutions against their critics. The extreme to which criminal libel was carried was reflected in an historic debate in England in 1792. An instance was put where criminal libel was filed against one who called a man "a great bore." "He put the case, that an action for a libel was brought for using a modern word, not to be found in any grammar or glossary, *viz.* for saying that a man was 'a great bore'; a jury would laugh at such a ground of prosecution, but the judges would turn to their grammars and glossaries, and not being able to meet with it, would say they could not find such a phrase as 'a great bore,' but they had found a wild boar, which no doubt it meant; and yet it could not be, as a wild boar had four legs, and a man was a two-legged animal; then it must mean, that the plaintiff was like a wild boar in disposition, which was a wicked libel, and therefore let the defendant be hanged."

Seditious libel and criminal libel greatly restricted the range of discussion of matters of public concern. They were a sword that hung over every speaker. A famous libel law was passed in England in 1789 giving the jury, rather than the judge, the power to determine what utterances were criminal. But juries are often victims of passion. The vital question is not who should determine what utterances are criminal. Far more important is what utterances are immune from prosecution. The common law and the British Sedition Act of 1798 made the casting of blame on government and its officials criminal because that might bring the existing regime into disrepute and result in its overthrow. The cry for reform was the abolition of laws that punished utterances that had a tendency, however remote, to undermine the state. The response in this country was the First Amendment, which provides that Congress shall make "no" law that abridges freedom of speech.

## Freedom of Speech and Communism

Those main historic currents have been carried into the modern stream of law. Last century the anarchists and socialists loomed on the scene as threats to the *status quo*. This century the Communists have taken their place; and the issue, though drawn in a different setting, has a familiar ring to those who know history.

Can the teaching of Marxist theory be constitutionally barred? Many may think as a matter of policy that Marxism should be taught in order to apprise the citizens of the nature of this ideological competitor on the world horizon. Others have thought that communism is too menacing as a movement, that Marxism has too corrupting an influence to be introduced into the classroom.

Will a community tolerate a school board that introduces Marxism into the curriculum of a high school? Will trustees revolt if a college or university faculty introduces it as a subject matter? Even if the powers-that-be protest, why should not students come to know what classical and modern Marxism is in theory and what in actuality it practices? How can communism be effectively combated as a creed if it is not known? Are not the dynamics of communism in underdeveloped nations, as related by Ward, *Five Ideas That Change the World,* highly relevant to our immediate problem?

Is there a constitutional difference when the teacher or speaker is a member of the party? A teacher or speaker who is not a Communist would doubtless give a more objective, dispassionate account of Marxism or Leninism than one who is a believer. But the First Amendment was designed for those who are passionate advocates as well as for those who are calm and objective in their discussion of ideas. The survey of Downs in *The First Freedom* makes that abundantly clear.

Why then can Communists be prosecuted for speaking about communism? One prosecution was for a conspiracy to teach Marxism. The element of conspiracy did not add to the gravity of the crime, for in that setting it meant no more than that several individuals had agreed to proselytize a creed. What was punished was still speech, not overt acts against the nation.

The maintenance of this prosecution marked a sharp break with American constitutional theory. We returned to the earlier British test of whether teaching a particular creed or speaking on a particular subject had a tendency to produce an illegal end. At first the American test was put in terms of a "clear and present danger" that the speech or utterance would produce the illegal end, which in this case was the forcible overthrow of the government by force and violence. But now the test was revised. There was no "clear and present danger" that the American Communist Party could in the 1940's or 1950's seize any post in government or otherwise get into control. The test, as revised, stated that the danger need not be "clear and present." Speech was punishable if it was the intent of the speaker to advocate the overthrow of the government "as speedily as circumstance would permit." See Fellman, *The Limits of Freedom*. We swung back not too far from the position of the early law which made treasonable the "compassing or imagining" the death of the king. The power of the words spoken—the danger that they might ignite the crowd and lead to violent overthrow—became irrelevant. It was the intent to advocate action that was critical.

Being an "active" member of the party was also made a crime. Being an "active" member was no more than believing in the Marxist doctrine and advocating it as a course of action. There was no element of taking action against the country in the sense of an overt act.

All speech is to a greater or lesser degree incitement to action or belief. The person who is an "advocate" of an unpopular political creed or who is "active" in promoting it is condemned not for the danger he creates but for the intent with which he utters his ideas.

The example given in justification is the shouting of "fire" in a crowded theatre. That, however, is an instance where speech and action are closely brigaded; that is an utterance that produces a riot. That is a classic example of "clear and present danger."

Punishment of those who advocate a form of government noxious to the majority is a departure from our constitutional theory. Those who collect arms or lay plots against the government have no claim to constitutional protection. But those who advocate noxious ideas merely offer them in the market to be accepted or rejected as men's reason or needs dictate. The suppression of the exposition or advocacy of a competing ideology (as we witnessed in the 1940's and 1950's) is not in line with the First Amendment.

## Loyalty oaths

Loyalty oaths have been fashionable in times of stress. During and after the Revolutionary War the hunt for "Royalists" was under way; and the loyalty oath was one device used against them. In the Civil War, Union commanders, as they advanced into the South, required the civilian populace to take loyalty oaths that they had not aided the South in the past and would not aid it in the future. Congress—and some states—went further and required officeholders, attorneys, and voters to take an oath that they had not aided the South. Refusal to take the oath made the person ineligible for the office or the calling, and deprived him of the right to vote. Those oaths—both federal and state—were held unconstitutional, *first*, because they imposed punishment by *ex post facto* laws, *i. e.* laws enacted after the offending act had been committed; and *second*, because they were bills of attainder, *i. e.* punishment imposed by the legislative branch rather than by the judiciary after a trial with the full protection afforded by the Bill of Rights.

The rash of loyalty oaths since World War II has reached farther into the lives of our people than at any other time. An oath required of a public servant to support the Constitution and to defend the country against all enemies, foreign and domestic, is essential, because one assuming a public post, even at the lower echelons, is a trustee and the people are entitled to his promise of fidelity. The loyalty oaths that have been challenged in recent days are quite different. As Chafee, *The Blessings of Liberty*, p. 162, points out, they create new grounds of ineligibility to engage in a person's work or calling—whether as public employee, attorney, street-car conductor, or boxer (and, under California law, even boy scouts who help out in a civil defense project of mass polio inoculation). These loyalty oaths disqualify a person for the position without any evidence being offered against him. His refusal to take the oath is the disqualification. Some elements in the oath may be utterly irrelevant to a person's present fitness for a particular job. He has to swear that he *never* was a member of the Communist Party. His membership may have been nominal. He may have joined with the idealistic notion that he could help produce a more humanitarian world, only to realize that the tactics employed by the party violated his principles. He may have joined innocently, and resigned when he realized the true nature of the party. Knowing full well the tactics and policies of the Communist Party, he may have joined it and later rebelled against it, being converted to the cause of the Free Society. No matter what the nature of his past membership, he is cast forever into the outer darkness. His engineering degree becomes worthless; his Ph.D. can get him admission to no college or university; a lifetime of training and experience go for naught because he once "sinned."

The case against him is more tenuous when it comes to another part of the modern test oath. For he usually must also swear that he never was a member of any association or group on the Attorney General's list or of any other association affiliated with the Communist Party. Here the injustice is even more pronounced.

First, the associations named by the Attorney General as "subversive" may or may not be such. No hearing was ever held. The Attorney General's determination that an organization was "subversive" was wholly *ex parte*.

Second, even if the Communists had infiltrated an organization, they may not have succeeded in using it for unlawful ends.

Moreover, many innocent people—interested in feeding refugees, getting reform measures passed, or setting up soup kitchens for unemployed people—may have joined the group wholly unaware that Communists had infiltrated it. Yet no matter how innocent they were, no matter how far removed they were from the

Communist taint, no matter how many years had passed since that affiliation, they were condemned by the modern test oath.

Insofar as the oath requires a person to swear he is not a member of the Communist Party, different considerations apply. If he is a knowing member of a group plotting to overthrow the government by force and violence, he deserves no place on the ballot nor in any responsible government post. Yet there may be many posts of a subordinate nature which do not involve work in a sensitive area. Complete outlawry of a person for an act or belief, not punished or punishable as a crime, is a throwback to the Dark Ages.

The degrees of membership vary from knowing and active to nominal or innocent. The modern test oath makes no distinction of that nature. Whether a person is a knowing and dangerous member or an innocent and harmless one is irrelevant to that oath. No matter the quality of present membership, the oath may be used, the courts say, to condemn the employee. Moreover, past membership or affiliation can be reached by the oath, provided it was not innocent. If the oath is drawn in terms of "knowing" past membership or affiliation, it can cast a person into the outer darkness, no matter how much he despises the Communist creed today.

Those people who once were members of the Communist Party did not commit a crime. Being a member was not made criminal until recently; and even then one had to be an "active" member who "advocated" Marxism to be punishable. Thus people, who were never convicted of a crime and could not be, were treated worse than felons. For while society attempts to rehabilitate convicted felons, it refuses redemption to anyone who once was a "knowing" member of the party even though his membership lapsed years ago and he is today a "convert" against communism.

The modern test oath thus outlaws or punishes a person without the constitutional procedures designed to protect him. As already noted, the Fifth Amendment requires an indictment returned by the grand jury, a trial before a petit jury, the right to counsel, and the right to have the accusing witness confront the accused. The modern test oath, like the old oath *ex officio*, provides a short cut that dispenses with those requirements. The citizen is condemned merely by refusal to take the oath. The oath, insofar as it punishes past conduct which at the time it was committed was not unlawful, is in effect an *ex post facto* law.

## Legislative investigations

The expression "Fifth Amendment Communist" also acquired currency during these last few decades. The Fifth Amendment has several clauses, including one that prohibits the confiscation of private property for public use. Private property taken for public use must be paid for. The Self-Incrimination Clause provides that no person "shall be compelled in any criminal case to be a witness against himself." That clause, like the one prohibiting confiscation of property, is anti-Communist in philosophy. It has, indeed, been common throughout history for totalitarian regimes to use force and coercion—either crudely or subtly—in making people confess to their crimes. The long periods of detention *incommunicado* in Russia are notorious. One of the historic struggles in the evolution of the Free Society was to require officials to be respectful of man's dignity, to get rid of the rack, the thumbscrew, and other methods of torture, and to use against an accused only those confessions which were voluntarily made. The Self-Incrimination Clause of the Fifth Amendment is a product of that experience. Here again, if government can force a person to speak, it can dispense with the time-consuming procedures of collecting evidence against him and persuading a grand jury to indict and a petit jury to convict. Men have short memories and at times forget that the Bill of Rights deliberately made it difficult for government to bring its awesome powers to bear against the citizen.

Though every person has a civic responsibility to cooperate with his government in enforcing the laws, he need not discuss any event or act which might implicate him in a crime. He has the privilege by reason of the Fifth Amendment to remain silent even as respects a single aspect of the incriminating act. For the law is that, if he talks about one item or link, he waives the privilege.

He may, however, be willing to talk about his own part but unwilling to implicate others. To what extent is he privileged to remain silent? Can he be sent to prison for refusing to be a tattle-tale? Even the late Senator McCarthy, when a witness, refused to divulge the source of his information, as Chafee, *The Blessings of Liberty* discloses. Is the ordinary citizen equally privileged?

He may think that the matter into which the committee is inquiring is not pertinent. Could a committee authorized to investigate railroad rates inquire into a witness's Communist affiliations? Certainly not.

A committee, authorized to investigate communism, summons a person because he made a speech against the committee, urging people to write their Congressmen and ask that the committee be dissolved. In trying to arouse public opinion against the committee he was exercising his constitutional right of petition. May the committee investigate him for attempting to rally the public against it? The answer is in the affirmative. Yet, what happens to the right of petition guaranteed by the Constitution?

Any legislative committee—state or federal—has the authority to investigate for one or two reasons: (1) it may inquire into the manner in which the laws are being administered or enforced; and (2) it may investigate in order to ascertain whether additional legislation is necessary. By hypothesis, therefore, any legislative committee is confined to fields in which it is competent to legislate. Since neither Congress nor the states may legislate respecting religion, the questions, To what church do you belong? When was the last time you went to confession? Why did you change from Catholicism to Protestantism? are plainly irrelevant. A witness who refuses to answer those questions may not be punished. Likewise, since neither Congress nor the states may legislate respecting the press, the questions to a publisher, Why did you endorse the cultural exchange program with Soviet Russia? How many of your reporters have ever been or are members of the Communist Party? Why did you approve the reduction in last year's budget of the appropriation for the Pentagon? need not be answered.

## Freedom of speech

Questions concerning one's political ideology and one's expression of views on socialism, communism, fascism, or democracy would by the same token seem immune from legislative inquiry.

But the courts have held that speech that is aimed at causing the overthrow of government "as speedily as circumstances permit" (even though that time is measurable only by decades rather than hours or days) may be investigated. Hence the legislature may investigate to see if there is an advocacy or an exposition of ideas aimed at an illegal objective "as speedily as circumstances permit."

Thus although freedom of the mind is protected by the First Amendment, the advocacy, teaching, and exposition of certain ideas is subject to regulation. Since they may be regulated, they may be investigated. Thus the roving inquiry into men's beliefs has become established on this continent, and one aim of the First Amendment has been defeated.

The exposition of ideas in the private sector, as for example denouncing an individual as a thief or a Communist, poses a different problem. If the quarrel or dispute is a family matter or involves a personal altercation, punishment of the speaker through a libel or slander action to collect damages for the wrong falls in the category of a private remedy for a strictly private injury. If damages may be collected for injury to a man's yard, why may they not be collected for injury to a man's reputation?

Congress could not pass a libel or slander law because the prohibition of the First Amendment against a federal law that abridges freedom of speech is in terms absolute. May the states enact such laws? They have done so from the beginning. When, of course, the Fourteenth Amendment was adopted at the end of the Civil War each state was barred from depriving any person of "life, liberty or property" without Due Process. The Due Process Clause of the Fourteenth Amendment has been held to incorporate the First Amendment. That is to say, it is a denial of "liberty" without Due Process for a state to penalize a person for speaking. Can a state penalize a speaker for a libel or slander without violating Due Process? There are some who think the Fourteenth Amendment took that power from the states. Others say that the long history of libel and slander in the laws of the states indicates that if those actions were abolished by the Due Process Clause of the Fourteenth Amendment, a more explicit indication of the purpose would be found. If the latter view is correct, freedom of speech is more restricted when it comes to the states than it is when Congress is legislating.

However that may be, libel and slander liberally construed can be disastrous in a Free Society. If the man denounced as a thief is an officeholder entrusted with public funds, how can a ban be placed on a discussion of his honesty consistently with the enlightened exercise of the franchise? If every charge of dishonesty or corruption or venality leveled against an officeholder can lead to a suit for damages against the accused, the political processes would be greatly crippled. Truth, of course, is a defense. But charges and countercharges in the heat of a campaign are often exaggerated; and it may take a fortune to establish a defense. Unless there is the widest possible leeway in the discussion of public issues, the principle of "the consent of the governed" that underlies our political institutions would suffer. As a result, the laws of libel and slander have been ameliorated by the doctrine of "fair comment" which gives leeway to those debating or exposing public issues, so that they may not be hauled into court by the heels even when their charges are false.

There are, however, limits. The British make criminal the use in a public place of abusive or insulting words which are designed to provoke a breach of the peace and which do occasion it or are likely to do so. Somewhat the same rule obtains here. Thus the use of "fighting words" in public discourse is punishable. In those instances speech is so close to unlawful conduct as to be considered a part of it.

## Censorship

Censorship prior to publication was practiced in England prior to 1695 when the last licensing system for the press (excluding the stage) expired. That kind of prior restraint has been tried here; but it has been uniformly said to be violative of the First Amendment when it concerns newspapers or speakers. But a different rule has emerged as respects movies. When it comes to movies, the argument that *all* prior restraints are infringements of the First Amendment's guarantee of freedom of speech and press has been given only lip service.

Any system that requires an administrative hearing and determination as a condition to the free expression of ideas would seem to be an unconstitutional invasion of First Amendment rights, though literature expressing the contrary view is plentiful. See Gardiner, *Catholic Viewpoint on Censorship*. It could, indeed, lead to eventual censorship of every form of communication, be it newspapers, books, magazines, television, radio, or public speeches.

Censorship of the publication or distribution of literature is an evil power. By a stroke of the pen a movie or a tract can be banned, an editorial cancelled, a news item altered, or a speech changed in quantity, quality, or emphasis. With that kind of a system in vogue, publishers, authors, speakers are under the censor's thumb. If they disagree with his ruling, they can take him into court. But months might pass before a decision overruling the censor is obtained. By then the election will be over or the occasion for the editorial or the speech forgotten. These are the practical reasons why the censor's rule is insufferable.

Punishment for movies released, speeches made, editorials written, or news comments published also has a powerful deterrent effect. Yet punishment after the event entails the use of procedural safeguards in the Bill of Rights—trial by jury, the right to confront opposing witnesses, an appeal to a more distant tribunal in case of conviction, and a ruling on constitutional rights in a chamber removed from the scene of controversy.

Movie censorship in this country has not involved political ideology. Rather, it has been almost entirely concerned with obscenity. While movie censorship has been upheld, censorship of other parts of the press has been struck down.

Both in movies and in literature generally, obscenity has concerned itself with two aspects of sex. First is the school of thought that condemns a play, a movie, a novel, or other publication because it arouses lustful thoughts and desires. Many plays, books, and magazines have been banned because they contained passages offensive to someone in the Post Office Department or to some Purity League that had influence with a censorship board or with a prosecutor. Finally the rule emerged from court decisions that it was the character of the book as a whole, not isolated passages, by which it was to be judged.

But should a publication whose main impact is the arousal of sexual desires be banned? A goodly part of life is the arousal of sexual desires.

It is said that youth needs protection against books and articles that arouse sexual desires. But we know from researches in this age-old field that sex literature is not an important factor in arousing youth's sexual desires. Adults are the ones most afflicted, and men more than women. The male who is commonly aroused is an adult in the upper social groups. So the desire to protect either juveniles or society turns out to be a pretense.

The real purpose is to make the public live up to the censor's code of morality. The vice of the test that makes arousal of sexual appetites a basis for condemning a book, an article, or a movie is that it enables one censor, who is a prude, to ban Shakespeare or even *The Song of Solomon,* while it enables another to follow blindly the list of banned books which some group has at hand.

Sex cannot be suppressed in life. Should it be attempted in literature?

The law has not quite reached the point of answering the question in the negative. The American test is today expressed in other terms. Stories of sex can be told, it is said, unless they have no appeal except to a prurient interest. The text is to be judged, it is said, for its effect upon normal people in the community, not upon members particularly susceptible.

If nothing could be published that might appeal to some person's prurient interest, then the entire community would be reduced to the reading level in the sex field of that, say, of the anal erotic group. When a state actually barred the distribution of books found to have a "potentially deleterious influence on youth," the statute was struck down as reducing the adult population to reading only what is fit for children. Banning books that appeal to anal erotics would treat all adults as sick and unable to withstand exposure to the world of ideas.

What appeals to the "prurient" interest? The answer usually given is "filth" or "pornography." What is "pornography"? Not literature which contains four-letter words or smut. That would condemn even the writings of the late William Faulkner. One test is whether the work has any literary value or whether its dominant appeal is to the prurient interest. There is room for differences of opinion even when that test is applied.

The major current controversy in the field of obscenity is over procedural matters.

First, what standards should be applied? In cases of movie censorship, state licensing systems that provide standards so vague as to leave the censor at large have been held invalid.

In a recent case a license was required before a film could be shown, and the license would be issued only if the censor in his discretion approved. The standards were not in issue, only the censor's discretion. That power is as obnoxious to the Free Society as is the power of a police officer to seize any magazine which the officer thinks is obscene. The same is true respecting novels, poems, and other tracts. Officers—whether postal or otherwise—must act by definite legal standards, not by their own whim or caprice.

One state statute permitted local police officers to obtain search warrants for obscene materials solely upon an affidavit that the offending dealer or distributor was in possession of books or magazines that *the officers deemed obscene.* The judge or magistrate to whom the application was made was not required to make an independent determination of obscenity, nor need he be shown a sample of the offending books or magazines. The Court held that apart from the fact that no opportunity was afforded the distributor or dealer to contest the officer's assertion of obscenity prior to the issuance of the warrants, the state could not permit seizures based only upon the individual judgment of a police officer that certain matters were obscene. Nor may a private group lawfully combine with a prosecutor to bring proceedings against a retailer or a publisher and impose by law that particular group's code of morality. A private group, such as a church, can of course use all its powers of persuasion to keep its members from reading books which it deems harmful. But church and prosecutor together cannot ban books, and impose their moral code on the community. Yet private groups at times frighten booksellers into keeping books from their shelves. This tactic is used not only against tracts deemed obscene because of the sex content. It is also used against other literature. Thus in Washington, D.C. a private group recently intimidated a chain store that sells paperbacks from distributing *The Dead Sea Scrolls* by the late

A. Powell Davies because the book has heretical overtones.

Second, what procedures for condemning obscene publications satisfy Due Process? The procedures used are often as important as the standards to be applied. Particularly is this true where distribution of the material is made to turn upon an *ex parte*, nonjudicial determination of obscenity by an administrative official. The postal authorities undertake to exclude obscene literature from the mails, though there has been no final decision sustaining their power to do so solely upon an *ex parte* determination.

Judicial, as well as administrative, procedures must be fair. Thus the statute or judge-made rule is defective if it does not require a prompt determination of the issue of obscenity. In some states the court is not required to reach a decision on the merits within any particular time, although it is required to afford the aggrieved party a hearing within 20 days after the seizure. The evil of that procedure was illustrated in a case where two months had elapsed between the seizure and the state court's decision. During that time some 180 publications, later found not obscene, had been suppressed and withheld from the market.

One state procedure was upheld and the distribution of specific publications was enjoined pending a hearing to determine their obscenity, where the injunction was limited to a particular magazine or book before the court, where a trial on the merits was required to be held within one day after the joinder of issue, and where a decision had to be rendered not more than two days after the conclusion of the trial.

The critical procedural area is that dealing with prior nonjudicial restraints, where the issue of obscenity is tried by a local official acting in an administrative capacity. There the power to delay a decision, magnified by slow-moving processes of judicial review, becomes the power to destroy, and, unless closely supervised, results not only in economic death for the publisher or distributor, but in the demise of free expression as well.

## Challenging the status quo

Science produces a constantly changing technology that may make an engineer's education obsolete in a decade. Those changes are accepted as "progress" though they bring tragedy to some. We do not have the same objectivity in relation to ideas in other fields.

The struggle of man to be unafraid of ideas has marked human history. The conventional has always plagued us; it has conditioned us to one way of thinking. Our prejudices become rooted in folklore.

The curious man—the dissenter—the innovator—the one who taunts and teases or makes a caricature of our prejudices is often our salvation. Yet throughout history he has been burned or booed, hanged or exiled, imprisoned or tortured, for pricking the bubble of contemporary dogma.

The writer and the thinker are the ones who frequently show that a current attitude is little more than witchcraft. They may do in art, in business, in literature, in human relations, in political theory what Darwin did with biology, Freud and Jung with the subconscious, Einstein and Rutherford with physics. This folklore or mythology by which we all live needs challengers, doubters, and dissenters lest we become prisoners of it. We need those who provoke us so that we may be warned of the fate that our prejudices or ignorance or wishful thinking may hold in store for us. It was Keynes, I believe, who said that "the difficulty lies, not in the new ideas, but in escaping from the old ones."

Ideas are more dangerous than armies. Ideas have immortality, ideas cross impassable frontiers, ideas penetrate any Maginot line of conformity. Voices can be stilled; men and women imprisoned; books burned. But their ideas live on to torment the executioners, jailers, and censors.

It was a tumult and a clash of ideas, speeches, arguments, and debate, challenge and counter-challenge that hammered out on the anvil of public debate all structural and substantive features of our form of government. The question whether the Constitution should be adopted was a see-saw contest of opposed ideas. Separation of church and state was a narrowly-won victory. Then, as now, there were those who wanted religious groups to keep their fingers in affairs of state. We started, indeed, as a congeries of states with theocratic creeds, much in the fashion of Pakistan and Saudi Arabia today. The struggle of the churches to maintain control and the gradual secularization of government should be an oft-told tale; but it has largely been forgotten by laymen.

The passionate arguments in colonial days over religious affairs changed to economic and political matters after our central government was established. The new struggle was between ideas of federalism projected into what has come to be known as the common market and the opposing idea of states' rights—an argument that Marshall largely won as against Jefferson, but that continues in a measure today.

The problems of the central bank, high interest rates and low prices for agricultural products, sweatshops for women and children, rates charged by public utilities, factory conditions and hours of work, trade unionism, strikes, lockouts and boycotts, price control, guarantee of bank deposits, private or public control of atomic energy, private or public control of outer space—all these issues and hundreds more have been hammered out in public discussions. Those who challenged *laissez-faire* capitalism were the heretics of last century—the socialist or anarchist or other "subversive."

Issues have changed but the lines remain drawn between the *status quo* on one side and change on the other. At home the new *status quo* is the product of yesteryear's reformers but the new critics do not necessarily advocate a return to earlier days. Though they want change, their change is not, for example, the abolition of the Interstate Commerce Commission but improvement in administrative procedures. Farm economies have been built into closed societies. The beneficiaries who raise wheat, cotton, and corn, have established empires; and to change or alter those empires to meet world or domestic conditions is like remaking the feudal map of Europe in the 15th century.

The phenomenon common to every age has been the demand for change. Without the freedom to expose the failings and abuses and frustrations of the *status quo*, existing conditions would be or become insufferable. For while man has gained much in knowledge during the known years of civilization, it is doubtful if he has gained much in wisdom. Base, selfish interests dominate today as they did in the days when Mesopotamia was first made fertile. The major achievement of the Free Society is in the ability to change the *status quo* without violence, to cast a current practice into limbo and adopt a new one by an election, to remake the economy or renovate an institution, yet not destroy it, to refashion even the structure of government by votes rather than by force.

Yet revolution is our tradition and the tradition of the Western World. Revolution by force is one of our people's reserved rights memorialized in the Declaration of Independence. But persuasion, not force, is our preferred way.

Abroad, the *status quo* in many nations is feudalism that must be displaced. The complex of forces described by Barbara Ward in *Five Ideas That Change the World* is vast and complicated. To see what on the one hand is crass and vulgar and corrupt abroad and on the other noble and inspired requires discernment that comes only with knowledge of the facts and much debate. To attribute virtue to all that is anti-Communist is to chant a litany without real meaning. Without debate on foreign issues and policy we become prisoners of those who manipulate opinion. Yet when has there been debate on foreign policy issues? Who knows what basic policies the rulers whom we have kept in power stand for? Who knows what sums of money they have banked abroad out of our grants or loans? What ideas of freedom and justice have we been promoting in the Middle East, in Asia, in Latin America? The masses of people in the world clamor for change in their *status quo*. It will come with blood as in Cuba or by law as in India. Yet we, who have virtually shut off debate on these vital overseas issues, are not prepared for the shock and disillusionment to come. We are not at ease with ideas. We have forgotten our revolutionary heritage. We have identified our *status quo* with the public interest of the world, when, indeed, we are the white house on the hill surrounded by the slums. How can we get on a wave length with the people who inhabit the slums? Can their idea of the good life approximate ours? Are not India and Israel closer to their comprehension than we? We are rich and powerful. But absent of ideas that touch the commun humanity of all men, we live in haughty isolation.

The safety of the Republic lies in unlimited discourse. Only when the mind is free to explore problems to the horizon is man free to challenge and criticize intelligently those in power and summon an opposition to depose them. Debate which can be cut off or throttled is, of course, better than no debate at all. Yet debate should reach entrenched rights and expose them and point the way to a new freedom. The desirability of unlimited debate is commonly expressed in terms of the search for truth. The search for the bacillus that produces a virus is a search for truth. So is the search for the anatomy of the atom and outer space. Yet what should be done about all those discoveries and how they should be used are not matters of truth but of safety or expediency. Destruction of the bacillus may cure one or more million men; but it may leave them easy prey to other bacilli. Atomic energy unleashed on the world means the end of life. Outer space may be the handmaiden to that destruction.

The truth in these situations is elusive. It is, indeed, chameleonlike, depending on value judgments. Those who think they have the secrets of the good life may classify all who are opposed as the enemy and be willing to use the atomic bomb to destroy the enemy. Those who see good, as well as bad, in a diversity of politics, economics, and religion may be willing to scrap the bomb for simpler ways of life.

One of the leading Catholics of our time, Rt. Rev. John J. Considine, recently stated the concern that all must have for the needs and aspirations of all men: "All Christians according to their state have a duty to speak for justice among all men throughout the planet and the delegation to act in fraternal charity for all men throughout the planet." But with missionary zeal he says, "The Christian should contemplate and appraise the false ideas that other men believe but not in arrogance and disdain. We approach all mankind, believer and unbeliever, not to condemn them but to gain them." A Presbyterian, or Baptist, a Zen Buddhist or a Moslem, a Hindu or a Bahai may likewise think that he has a monopoly on the "truth" and that all other ideas are "false." Freedom of the mind encourages the right to believe in one creed or dogma or system passionately and devotedly. He who embraces any such belief, whether it is a systematic creed or only a generalized conception of God, or a godless world is sovereign in his right to proclaim what to him is the "truth." To deny his "truth" may in his eyes be sinful. To say therefore that the search for "truth" is not man's mission may seem to some to be the ultimate sin. But those who construct a political system on the basis of their "truth" create totalitarianism. Those who passionately believe in democracy, like Father Considine, leave room for all searchers of "truth" and never impose by law one doctrine, one creed, one dogma, one faith on anyone. The struggle of men has been to create political institutions which prevent government from putting its imprimatur on what the majority or those in power may conceive to be the "truth." In that sense the problem of our age is not to discover "truth" but to accommodate conflicting views of "truth" and the common good or conflicting needs.

Is American mass production better for India than cottage industries?

How much of our natural resources should be converted into dollars? How much into spiritual values?

What room should be left for the Thoreaus, the Muirs, the Whitmans? What room for the loggers?

Should birth control be a debatable matter? Should government finance a birth control program?

If immoral literature or immoral movies are to be banned, who is to be the judge of "morality"? Is a Freudian standard to be adopted? Or a Victorian one? Or if the clergy are to decide, what sect?

To what extent should drug addicts be treated as criminals? To what extent as sick people?

The people cannot be informed and intelligent voters if government operations are kept secret. What should be disclosed? What should be made public? Who should decide?

The list is long and endless. Truth is not the goal, for in most areas no one knows what truth is. The search is for a way of life that offers the individual the greatest possible opportunity for fulfillment. The goal may change from age to age; or even if it remains constant, the means of achieving it may need revision as, for example, when automation produces vast unemployment or when the need to keep a critical foreign nation out of one political orbit means giving it trade preferences which have severe repercussions at home.

There are always watchmen who rally the city fathers, the state legislature, or the board of education to fasten their religious code or their moral code on the community. There have been many Anthony Comstocks who have mutilated freedom and left society paralyzed with prejudices that hamper free inquiry.

Freedom of the mind does not exist long unless it has outspoken sponsors who make free inquiry and free expression their cause.

These sponsors need not be advocates of a particular ideology. Indeed every one who proselytizes one creed or faith is apt to have a list of heretics whom he pursues and whom he would crush, if he could. The true sponsors of the Free Society are those who defend the advocates of creeds they despise.

In theory we trust the common sense or informed judgment of people to listen to opposed views and select what they think is the preferred course. The making of these value decisions is supposed to be left to the masses after full debate and discussion. If there is someone at the controls who, as censor, refuses to let some ideas be expressed, if prosecutors are free to pursue promoters of offending ideas, if the newspaper publisher prints (or the radio or TV announces) only the news that fits the owner's party line, the debate and discussion become truncated and the people become a captive audience.

It is not surprising that that is our condition today. The problems are so vast and they have been tumbling at us so fast that, even if we were worldly-wise and sophisticated, we would have trouble keeping abreast. Given our predilection to provincialism and to conformity, given the conservative class that controls the mass media of communication, we have become polarized to the right of center and assert the prerogatives of power to channel public discussion here and discourage it elsewhere. We have become the new conservatives who, unlike the old, practice intolerance.

If we are to have freedom of the mind in America, we must produce a generation of men and women who will tower above the press, as well as the crowd, and make tolerance for all ideas the symbol of virtue.

# What to read
## on freedom of the mind

Fellman, David. *The Limits of Freedom*. New Brunswick, N.J., Rutgers University Press, 1959. 144 p. $2.75.

In this book, the author discusses three important areas of the First Amendment: the relationship between church and state; the limitations placed on freedom of expression by state and federal laws and by judicial decisions; and, lastly, the right to talk politics (a phase of free speech) and the limitations placed on it when ideas deemed "subversive" are being advanced. This small book stirs many controversial issues and offers several explanations as to why the Bill of Rights has been construed to mean something less than it says.

Douglas, William O. *The Right of the People*. Garden City, N.Y., Doubleday, 1958. 238 p. $4.00.

This book is in three parts. The first deals with freedom of expression under the First Amendment. There is some history, some philosophy, but mostly analyses of the major constitutional decisions dealing with restraints on free speech. The second part deals with the right of privacy that has radiations not only from the Fourth and Fifth Amendments but from the First as well. Investigations of opinions and belief, guilt by association, loyalty investigations, the "test" oaths in their modern garb, self-incrimination, searches and seizures, wire tapping, the use of torture and other more subtle means of coercion—all these are treated in the second part. There is also included a discussion of the citizen's right to shake his fist at an unconstitutional statute, a modern right that stems from the Puritans who defied the English sovereign by adhering to their forms of worship.

The third part is concerned with the struggle in the Western World to keep the military under civilian control. Punishment of civilians by military tribunals was an early grievance of the British subject. The raising of a standing army in time of peace was also an ominous threat. The civilian authorities took over discipline of soldiers in time of peace. The common law of England did not recognize courts-martial. There are not many accounts of the evolution of civilian control on this continent. This one is not detailed, but the story is told in abbreviated form. There is a case by case account on this side of the water through the Civil War and in the era following World War II, when the American military reached for greater and greater power. The major constitutional decisions are summarized and discussed.

Gellhorn, Walter. *American Rights; the Constitution in Action*. New York, Macmillan, 1960. 232 p. $4.50.

This book contains eight chapters that delve deeply into constitutional decisions of the courts: habeas corpus, criminal procedures, freedom of speech, free speech and communism, freedom not to speak, legislative investigations, freedom of movement, and desegregation of public schools. There is a ninth chapter that deals with a very important but little discussed topic—the extent to which "private" groups constitute a form of government that limits the freedoms that the Constitution protects. The power of the corporation over the communities where it is located and of unions over their members and prospective employees is explored; also the control of a manufacturer over retail outlets, censorship of movies and literature by private groups, denial of membership in professional societies to certain racial groups, the responsibility of lessees of state properties to practice non-discrimination, and the refusal of business to deal with certain racial groups.

McKeon, Richard P., Robert K. Merton, and Walter Gellhorn. *Freedom to Read; Perspective and Program*. New York, R. R. Bowker, 1957. pap. 128 p. $1.25. (Published for the National Book Committee)

This book also treats the problem of censorship both by an official and by a private group. It argues that censorship is unsound, impractical, and undesirable on philosophic grounds, that its use must be restrained lest it impair freedom of expression, that its use is in any event not effective in achieving the ends it seeks to reach. Overall the book is first a plea for embracing the freedom to read by raising the level of reading tastes and by encouraging the creative, nonconforming artists and thinkers. Morality, it is claimed, is not advanced by restricting communication which only stimulates curiosity. The second plea is for studies which will show how censorship works, what its actual results are, what effect it is having on authors, and what standards state and federal governments use in selecting books for schools, libraries, etc.

Wiggins, James R. *Freedom or Secrecy*. New York, Oxford University Press, 1956. 242 p. $4.00.

Secrecy in governmental affairs has put an increasingly severe curb on public information available for public debate, discussion, and enlightenment. The result is that the people know less and less about their government. Some say it makes little difference, as the problems of government are so complex that only the expert can understand them anyway. That is the philosophy of despair. It also repudiates the basic thesis of our government that, given the right to know, the people can exercise their sovereign will intelligently.

The right to know is indeed the main purpose of the First Amendment, just as the opportunity to learn is the chief objective of the public school. Not everything can be disclosed, as diplomatic negotiations, delicate international affairs, and national security illustrate. But these excuses have often been pushed way beyond national ends; the press has become more and more dependent on press releases from government bureaus; and the public has been kept more and more in the dark on vital issues.

This book is a highly factual account by an acute observer on the national scene of the manner in which government works more and more for secrecy, and an appeal by an ardent advocate of the Free Society to the informed public for action. Some incidental sidelights are thrown on the main problem by illustrations of state laws designed to make the operation of state government more public and less secret.

**Chafee, Zechariah, Jr. *The Blessings of Liberty.* Rev. ed. Philadelphia, Lippincott, 1956. 350 p. $5.00.**

This is a highly accurate factual account of the forces in America that have been working toward conformity in thoughts and attitudes. The author, a late distinguished Harvard professor, gives an accounting of his forty-odd years with the problems of freedom of speech. He reviews the outstanding repressive legislative measures that have been passed; the denial of passports to one whose views were not liked; the work of the Customs Bureau and Postal Authorities in censoring books and magazines; the role of the State Department as censor of literature going overseas; Congressional committees (how one went so far as to condemn the notable film *The Best Years of Our Lives* because a banker balked at making a loan to a veteran); the loyalty and security-risk program and the manner of its operation; the use of the Attorney General's list to cast all sorts of people into the outer darkness; state loyalty programs that paralleled the federal one; the vast application of the "test" oath to a host of people.

The book, while it considers the constitutionality of laws trenching on freedom of speech and inquiry that have been passed, has its main emphasis on the question of their propriety, wisdom, and necessity. It shows how little was accomplished by the so-called "subversive" legislation—beyond arousing people to a white heat, and electing witch-hunters to office. It gives a revealing account of the manner in which Bar Associations were awakened to the danger when their members were also threatened with a "test" oath. If it could be required of teachers, why not of lawyers?

The book contains the best treatment I know of the problem of the *right not to speak*. The historical materials are treated in depth and the modern applications are shown. If a Senator could properly refuse to disclose his informants, why could an ordinary citizen be put to the wall for refusal to be a tattle-tale? An excellent account is given of religious liberty and the significance of separation of church and state and there is a philosophical discussion of the importance of the freedom to think, both to the individual and to society. There is no sentimentality in this chapter, only down-to-earth practicalities.

The two concluding chapters deal with liberty of expression in other areas of the world and the importance of free speech in welding nations together and of a free press in educating peoples of one nation to world needs. The book closes with a discussion of the manner in which the Western tradition can penetrate Eastern customs.

Konvitz, Milton R. *Fundamental Liberties of a Free People; Religion, Speech, Press, Assembly.* Ithaca, N.Y., Cornell University Press, 1958. 420 p. $5.00.

This book is exclusively devoted to the forty-five words that comprise the First Amendment. It deals in other words with three rights— the right of religion, of speech and press, and of assembly. Each of the three parts is a solid account that starts with the historic roots of the right in question and follows through to modern decisions.

The conflict between some religious exercises and the police power is discussed. Separation of church and state is considered and the meandering line marked by court decisions is traced. The place of private religious schools in a free society is analyzed. The freedom of churches from government control and the awful consequences if secular authority dominates ecclesiastical matters is shown.

The second part lumps together speech, press, and assembly. The freedom not to speak and the right to be let alone are discussed at length. Censorship, obscene literature, taxes on knowledge, "test" oaths, and loyalty oaths come in for separate and detailed treatment.

The third part of the book discusses the "clear and present danger" test that judges invented to justify punishment of free speech. Holmes, now thought of as the Great Defender, was the one who made the "clear and present danger" test articulate and used it to send to jail some puny objectors in World War I. The manner in which the test has been changed, watered down, and made a meaningless juridical chant is told in an accurate and impressive way.

An appendix that deals with the history of the adoption of the Bill of Rights and an array of footnotes makes the book a mine of information for the student.

Downs, Robert B. ed. *The First Freedom; Liberty and Justice in the World of Books and Reading*. Chicago, American Library Association, 1960. 469 p. $8.50.

There is a vast literature on freedom of speech and of press and Robert B. Downs has collected much of it in this volume. One who undertakes this task makes his selections with a standard in mind. The communist school has been in favor of censorship so that people will have the "correct thoughts." Facist groups have taken the same stand. Some churches have done the same. So has every dictator who held power. One in favor of censorship would have rich material varying from Soviet directives and papal edicts, to speeches by ministers of education under totalitarian regimes. Mr. Downs, being a trustee of the Free Society, makes no such selection. His selection of materials, whether on censorship, political subversion, pressure groups, obscenity, or police surveillance of literature, is made with an eye to the values represented in the First Amendment.

The result is no monotonous flow of essays. A wide variety of views is offered. The developing law under the First Amendment has produced a contrariety of schools of thought. These are all represented. D. H. Lawrence on *Pornography and Obscenity* is not separated by many pages from the distinguished Jesuit, John Courtney Murray, on *Literature and Censorship*.

Schools, the mails, the libraries, the press, book burning, the work of pressure groups, leading court opinions (majority and dissents) are among the current problems covered. There is historical depth as well as the contemporary view in the papers offered. Censorship in China in 231 B.C., the burning of pagan literature by Christians in 389 A.D., the great epistles on freedom of the press from the English-speaking world, modern decisions—these are parts of the stream of history showing the endless efforts of rulers to control the minds of men. There are penetrating accounts of voluntary groups such as the National Organization for Decent Literature which, like Anthony Comstock of an earlier day, seeks to take the law into its hands. There is testimony in a censorship case, philosophical discussions of the censor's role, sarcastic and biting accounts of repressive practices, articles of faith about America and the First Amendment, and ringing calls to action by those who really care about the Free Society.

There are twelve chapters in all. One is entitled "Censorship in Ireland"; another is named "Books under dictators red and black." These two alone are worth the price of the volume. It makes one who loves freedom have sleepless nights to hear what often goes on under the name of religion or the necessity for law and order.

Carson, Rachel. *Silent Spring*. Boston, Houghton, Mifflin, 1962. 368 p. $5.00.

At first blush this may seem to be out of place in a series dealing with *Freedom of the Mind*, for it is a book on insecticides. It tells the mounting toll of life which insecticides exact. Five hundred new ones a year appear; and they upset the bone ecology of the earth. Fish, birds, humans are threatened.

Where is the truth about these dazzling and attractive poisons to be found? Why do not our health officials rave and rant? Why do not prosecutors use such laws as they have to halt these mass distributions of poison? Why are not crusades launched for new laws?

These questions give the reason why the book is relevant to the topic of freedom. We have a free press but the annual output of poisons increases. Where are the muckrakers of old? Why does not the TV commercial that shows these sprays in attractive form disclose their danger—to children through the milk they drink, to the parents through the lettuce in their salads, to the robin and bald eagle, and to the fish whose waters now contain lethal doses?

Gardiner, Harold C., S.J. *Catholic Viewpoint on Censorship*. Garden City, N.Y., Doubleday, 1958. 192 p. $2.95. pap. Image Books D125. 75¢

Gardiner presents the philosophical view for censorship to the end that the well-being of society will be served if certain ideas are curbed. The problems raised center primarily (though not exclusively) on obscenity. Some legal materials are used, but the primary materials are canon law and commentaries on it. The work of the National League of Decency and the National Office for Decent Literature is discussed. The Appendix contains five statements of opposing views on censorship made by five prominent writers or groups.

Ward, Barbara. *Five Ideas That Change the World*. New York, Norton, 1959. 188 p. $3.95.

Lady Jackson—known as Barbara Ward to her American audience—has written a number of books dealing with the interplay of West and East, the breakdown of feudalism in the East, the dynamics of international communism in the underdeveloped nations, the policies needed in the West if the tide is to be turned, and the economics and politics involved in the turning. The present volume is composed of lectures, given at University College in Ghana, concerning five main currents in world thoughts.

The first is nationalism, which is treated historically as well as in the modern setting where the main problem is a place in the sun for minorities. The second is industrialism—the transfer of people from the land to the cities, the evolution of private enterprise, socialism, communism, and other methods of centralized control. The third is colonialism that still casts its shadow over the various continents, for, though the colonial power left, neo-colonialism in the form of trade and alliances persists. The fourth is communism, which has been so bitterly denounced that it is hardly understood in its ramifications. The fifth is internationalism—an account of man's last hope to achieve through a rule of law freedom from destruction at the hands of his own technology.

This provocative book shows in general outline world conditions as they affect the masses; and it should sound the alarm at any attempt to put the world into groups of "we" and "they," "good" and "bad." Those who want to stomp out the "bad" will try first to shackle the mind. Those who see that we of this planet make up only one community will want unlimited scope for free inquiry.

Lacy, Dan. *Freedom and Communications.* Urbana, Illinois, University of Illinois Press, 1961. 93 p. $3.00.
This book is a thoughtful analysis of the complex factors which affect the communication of ideas. The mass media of communication, dependent directly or indirectly on a huge mass audience, resistant to change, tends to lean toward overemphasis on predominant majority views; to conform to mediocre standards of taste. One result is that large numbers of citizens do not have easy access to new ideas and points of view, critical analyses of public affairs, or newer trends in art or literature. Thus the freedom to know, to make intelligent decisions on matters of public concern, to broaden one's background and deepen one's knowledge as a basis for making judgment of values is curtailed.